EXPLORING THE SOLAR SYSTEM

JUPITER

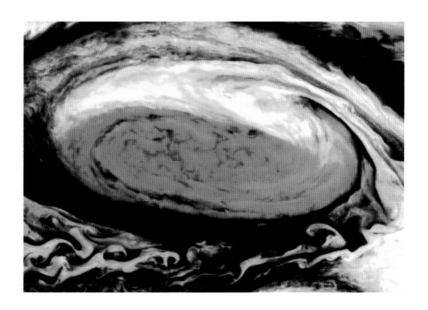

GILES SPARROW

Heinemann Library
Chicago, Illinois

JUPITER

Published by Heinemann Library,
an imprint of Reed Educational & Professional Publishing,
100 N. LaSalle, Suite 300, Chicago, IL 60602
Customer Service 888-454-2279
Visit our website at www.heinemannlibrary.com

Produced by Brown Partworks
Project Editor: Ben Morgan
Deputy Editor: Sally McFall
Managing Editor: Anne O'Daly
Designer: Steve Wilson
Illustrator: Mark Walker
Picture Researcher: Helen Simm
Consultant: Peter Bond

© 2001 Brown Partworks Limited

Printed in Singapore

06 05 04 03 02 01
10 9 8 7 6 5 4 3 2 1

Library of Congress Cataloging-in-Publication Data

Sparrow, Giles.
  Jupiter / Giles Sparrow.
      p. cm. -- (Exploring the solar system)
Includes bibliographical references and index.
  ISBN 1-57572-395-6
  1. Jupiter (Planet)--Juvenile literature. [1. Jupiter (Planet)] I.
Title.
  QB661 .S66 2001
  523.45--dc21
                                        00-010438

BELOW: *The planets of the solar system, shown in order from the Sun:*
Mercury, Venus, Earth, Mars, Jupiter, Saturn, Uranus, Neptune, Pluto.

CONTENTS

*Some words are shown in bold, **like this**.*
You can find out what they mean by looking in the glossary.

Where Is Jupiter?

Jupiter is the fifth planet from the Sun, after Mercury, Venus, Earth, and Mars. It is the closest of the gas giants—the huge planets made up almost entirely of gas that dominate the outer solar system. Beyond Jupiter lie the gas giants Saturn, Uranus, and Neptune, and finally icy Pluto, the smallest and outermost planet.

Massive Jupiter is the largest planet in the solar system. It is bigger than all the other planets put together and 1,300 times larger than Earth alone. With its family of 16 moons, some as big as planets, the Jupiter system is like a small solar system in its own right.

Like all the planets in the solar system, Jupiter moves around the Sun following a nearly circular path called an **orbit**. The time it takes to complete one orbit is the length of Jupiter's year, known as a **Jovian** year. Because Jupiter is much further from the Sun than Earth, its orbit is much longer, and a Jovian year lasts nearly twelve Earth years.

Getting to Jupiter

The time it takes to reach Jupiter depends on your method of transportation, and on the positions of Earth and Jupiter in their orbits when you set off.

Distance from Earth to Jupiter
Closest   **367 million miles (591 million km)**
Furthest   **600 million miles (965 million km)**

By car at 70 miles per hour (113 km per hour)
Closest   **600 years**
Furthest   **1,000 years**

By rocket at 7 miles per second (11 km per second)
Closest   **607 days**
Furthest   **992 days**

Time for radio signals to reach Jupiter (at the speed of light)
Closest   **33 minutes**
Furthest   **54 minutes**

Distance from the Sun

This diagram shows how far the planets are from the Sun. The exact distances vary a little over time because most planets orbit the Sun along slightly oval paths.

Sun   Mercury Venus Earth Mars   Jupiter   Saturn

0   **1,000 (1,609)**
Distance in millions of miles (kilometers)

Jupiter lies 483 million miles (778 million kilometers) from the Sun—about as far as you'd travel if you flew around Earth 20,000 times. But Jupiter's distance from Earth is continually changing and depends on the positions of the two planets in their orbits. They are closest when they line up on the same side of the Sun and furthest when they line up on opposite sides of the Sun.

Imagine you're about to join a **mission** to Jupiter. The journey will be very long—you will be away for about ten years. The spacecraft will be built in orbit around Earth, and will need to have some kind of **artificial gravity. Gravity** is the force that makes things fall to the ground on Earth. In space there is no gravity, so **astronauts** float in midair. This can be fun, but after a long time your bones and muscles would weaken from lack of exercise, so artificial gravity is necessary to keep you strong. Your spacecraft will also need lots of storage space—a crew of four needs more than 40,000 meals for a trip to Jupiter!

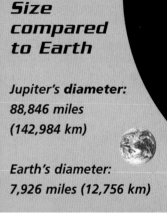

ABOVE: *The solar system is made up of the Sun, nine planets, and the asteroid belt. The planets travel around the Sun along paths called orbits.*

Size compared to Earth

Jupiter's *diameter:*
88,846 miles
(142,984 km)

Earth's *diameter:*
7,926 miles (12,756 km)

Uranus

Neptune

Pluto

2,000 (3,219)   3,000 (4,828)

First View

As you head toward Jupiter, it begins to look something like this photograph, taken from Earth using a small amateur telescope.

Your trip to Jupiter begins on board a space shuttle, which ferries you to a spacecraft waiting in orbit. The shuttle takes less than ten minutes to reach space.

It's time to set off. A space shuttle carries you into Earth's **orbit,** docks with the craft that will be your home for the next ten years, and you float into it through a connecting airtight passage. As the rocket engines fire up, the spaceship's acceleration creates **artificial gravity.** The rockets are designed to burn gently for a very long time—they don't have to blast the ship free of Earth's **gravity.** Midway through the journey the ship will turn around and, because the rockets are firing in the other direction, it will start to slow down. Although this means the trip will take longer, it saves fuel and gives you gravity right through the journey—zero gravity only happens when the spaceship is not speeding up or slowing down.

From Earth, Jupiter looks like a large, yellow star. At its closest to Earth it is brighter than any other object in the sky, apart from the Sun, our Moon, and Venus—our nearest neighboring planet. With binoculars or a small telescope, you can just make out Jupiter's circular shape, slightly squashed at the top and bottom, with four fainter stars close to it. These are Jupiter's four biggest moons, unique and fascinating worlds in their own right.

As the ship heads off, Earth and Moon begin to shrink in the window. About a year later you'll cross the orbit of Mars, and then the **asteroid belt. Asteroids** are huge lumps of rock, a few miles to hundreds of miles wide, orbiting the Sun between Mars and Jupiter. The belt is home to millions of asteroids, but they are spread out over such a big region of space that they are actually very far apart.

Getting Closer

Five years after setting off, you arrive at the Jupiter system. The journey has been long and dull, despite close glimpses of one or two asteroids. Jupiter has grown gradually brighter, and now its circular shape and the four bright moons can be clearly seen without a telescope. Approaching from one side, the planet appears as a **crescent,** with its brilliantly lit sunward face fading softly into the dense blackness of the dark side.

You can now see details on Jupiter's face: brown and cream stripes, and a big red spot. By watching the spot disappear and reappear as the planet **rotates,** you can make a rough guess at the length of a **Jovian** day—only ten hours. Despite being the solar system's largest planet, its day is the shortest.

Jupiter's moons are now visible as disks, dwarfed by the planet they orbit. One moon has cast a tiny shadow on Jupiter's face. You also notice flashes of light on Jupiter's dark side, and shimmering rings of light at the poles—like Earth, Jupiter has lightning and **auroras,** better known as northern and southern lights. Finally, the rocket engines turn off and the ship becomes silent. You are now floating in zero gravity, in orbit above Jupiter.

ABOVE: *Seen from the side, Jupiter appears as a crescent.*

RIGHT: *Close up, Jupiter's stripes are visible, along with the Great Red Spot on its lower half.*

Jupiter's Cloudscape

From your spectacular vantage point above Jupiter, the planet completely fills the sky. There is no land to be seen—just endless, swirling streams of clouds that are colored cream, brown, red, and occasionally blue. Jupiter's clouds are very different from those of Earth. They are not a thin covering over a rocky world below, but just the top layer in a ball of gas thousands of miles deep.

The biggest features on Jupiter are wide bands of clouds that encircle the planet, giving it a striped appearance. The clouds are stretched out this way by Jupiter's rapid **rotation**, which creates powerful high winds. After watching for a while you notice that neighboring bands of clouds seem to be moving in opposite directions, so some stripes appear to be moving backward. The boundaries between the bands look ragged, with colorful ripples and whirlpools where the clouds have swirled and mixed together.

Flying in for a closer look, you skim over the cloud tops and find that the upper clouds are nearly all cream-colored. Other colors appear where holes in the cream layer allow you to see down to the cloud layer below. The holes are created by areas of high pressure in the planet's **atmosphere.** On Earth, high pressure causes clear blue skies, while low pressure produces clouds and bad weather. The same principle applies on Jupiter, but here the high pressure just creates gaps in the top layer of clouds rather than completely clear skies.

*The Galileo **space probe** took this false-color photograph of Jupiter's swirling clouds. The white ovals are enormous storms.*

Life in the clouds

*Although Jupiter has no surface, some people have speculated that life might exist in the clouds. This artist's impression shows balloon-shaped animals like jellyfish being hunted by flying predators. Although this type of life might exist on a gas giant somewhere in the universe, **space probes** have shown that Jupiter lacks the chemicals needed for life.*

Brown and cream are the most common types of clouds on Jupiter, but there are others—blue clouds are located at the deepest levels of the planet's atmosphere, and red clouds can be found at even higher levels than the cream ones. Because Jupiter's atmosphere gets warmer as it gets deeper, the different cloud layers also match different temperatures—blue clouds are warmest, then brown and cream, and finally the uppermost red clouds, like the Great Red Spot, are the coldest.

*This computer-generated 3-D view across Jupiter's clouds was created from data sent to Earth by the **Galileo** probe. The blue area is a hole in the clouds.*

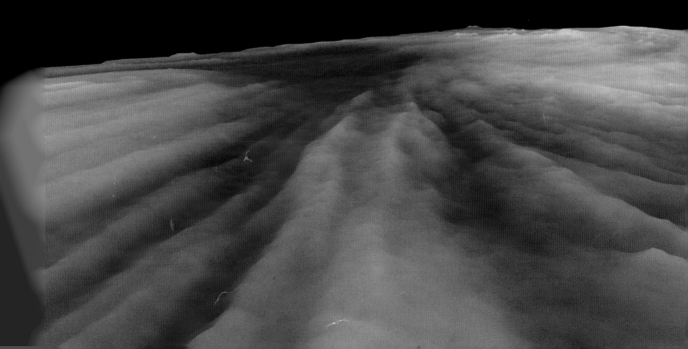

The Great Red Spot

Jupiter's Great Red Spot is a raging storm so gigantic that it could swallow Earth twice over. Like a hurricane on Earth, it spins around, sucking clouds into a vast whirlpool and generating ferocious winds. But in some ways the Spot is very different from a hurricane. As well as being much bigger and having faster winds, it refuses to die. Astronomers are baffled by this. The Great Red Spot has been seen for hundreds of years, and although it changes color and fades from time to time, it shows no sign of slowing down.

As well as being the biggest storm on Jupiter, the Great Red Spot is one of the highest features on the planet and is about five miles (eight kilometers) higher than the cream clouds around it.

ABOVE: *The Great Red Spot is about 16,000 miles (25,000 km) wide—more than twice Earth's diameter. Earth is shown here for comparison.*

Birth of a storm

Astronomers are only just beginning to understand how the Great Red Spot and other storms on the gas giant planets can form and survive for decades, or even centuries. There are long-lasting storms on both Saturn and Neptune, and the Great Red Spot itself has several neighboring white spots that have lasted more than 60 years.

By simulating cloud patterns in a laboratory, astronomers have shown that spinning areas in a gas giant's atmosphere tend to merge together to form a single large storm. In 1998, the Galileo spacecraft photographed two white storms (left) that later merged together in this way to form Jupiter's second biggest storm.

From your **orbit,** you can see that the Spot is much more than just a floating island of clouds—it devours other weather systems. As you watch, immense white clouds the size of North America drift toward the Spot, are swept up by the 250 mile per hour (400 kilometer per hour) winds, and are completely absorbed.

The Great Red Spot turns counterclockwise, taking about seven days to make one complete spin. It is always in the middle of the southern **hemisphere,** but it doesn't stay put. It races around Jupiter faster than the planet **rotates**, and it is constantly catching up with other clouds and swallowing them.

The Red Spot has different cloud levels: the highest are red and white, the lowest are blue and black.

Hurricanes on Earth

Earth's strongest hurricanes (left) have wind speeds of about 155 miles per hour (250 kilometers per hour), while the Great Red Spot moves at 250 miles per hour.

Heinrich Samuel Schwabe

(1789–1875)

The first person to draw the Great Red Spot on a map of Jupiter was the German astronomer Heinrich Samuel Schwabe, in 1831. However, the English physicist Robert Hooke was probably the first person to see it, nearly 200 years earlier.

13

What's Inside Jupiter?

You can't land on Jupiter because it doesn't have a solid surface. You could take a trip into the planet, but you'd never come back. Trapped by Jupiter's huge **gravity,** your spacecraft would keep falling until the enormous pressure of the **atmosphere** crushed the craft and everything inside it—including the crew. Eventually, you and your ship would melt and dissolve into Jupiter's atmosphere. Fortunately, astronomers can work out what's going on inside Jupiter without embarking on such a deadly **mission.**

hydrogen air

hydrogen and helium ocean

metallic hydrogen

core

Jupiter is mostly **hydrogen**—the same gas that the Sun is made of, and the most common **element** in the universe. In the upper region of the atmosphere the hydrogen is mixed with other chemicals, and these form Jupiter's clouds. The cloud layer extends only a short way into the planet—about 50 miles (80 kilometers) at most. Below it is a calmer inner region of hydrogen air, and below this is an ocean of liquid hydrogen and **helium** extending about a tenth of the way to the planet's center, or **core.** This strange ocean has no surface—it merges gradually into the air above.

The planet Jupiter has no real surface. Instead the atmosphere merges gradually from an outer region of mostly hydrogen clouds down to a hotter, thicker area of liquid hydrogen and helium.

The temperature and pressure rise steadily inside Jupiter as the hydrogen is squeezed ever tighter by gravity. Toward the bottom of the hydrogen ocean, strange things start to happen. In Jupiter's outer layers hydrogen exists as **molecules,** each made of two **atoms** joined together. Toward the planet's interior the molecules are broken apart by heat and pressure into a sea of individual atoms.

The hydrogen atoms act like liquid metal, so Jupiter's interior is like a huge globule of liquid mercury.

Set spinning by Jupiter's fast **rotation**, the metallic hydrogen generates an immense **magnetic field** around the planet that reaches all the way to Saturn and is 20,000 times more powerful than Earth's magnetic field. The intense magnetism traps deadly **radiation** near Jupiter. Unless your spacecraft was specially protected by radiation shields, Jupiter's magnetic field would kill you within minutes of entering it.

Jupiter's core is hotter than the surface of the Sun, but no one knows for sure what it is made of. It might be a ball of solid rock several times bigger than Earth, or perhaps the metallic liquid hydrogen goes all the way to the center.

In 1995 the Galileo *spacecraft released a probe that dived into Jupiter to study the planet's interior. The probe collected vital data before it was crushed by Jupiter's atmospheric pressure (artist's impression).*

Arthur C. Clarke
(born 1917)

In his 1985 novel 2010 (the sequel to the more famous 2001), science fiction author Arthur C. Clarke described an imaginary trip into the heart of Jupiter. He predicted that the planet's core might be pure carbon, compressed under enormous pressure to form a diamond the size of Earth.

How Jupiter Formed

Jupiter and the other gas giants are different from the planets of the inner solar system. They must have formed in different conditions, but it is not known exactly how.

All the planets were born about 4.5 billion years ago, shortly after the Sun itself started shining. The Sun formed from a huge gas cloud, the remains of which formed a disk of **debris** around the Sun. Clumps formed in the debris, and these clumps eventually became planets.

There are two rival theories to explain how Jupiter formed. In the first theory, ice and dust particles collided and built up to form a solid, Earth-sized **core,** which then pulled in gases with its **gravity.** According to the second theory, Jupiter formed from a huge region of gas that simply shrank by gravity. In either case, Jupiter would have been much bigger when it was forming.

Jupiter is about as big as a planet can get. If more material were added it wouldn't get much wider, it would just get more **dense.** Some people call Jupiter a failed star because it is made from the same ingredients as the Sun, but it isn't dense enough to generate the pressure needed to set it alight. In fact, Jupiter would need to weigh about 100 times more in order to turn into a star. It is more like a **brown dwarf**—a large object about twelve times heavier than Jupiter that shines dimly because of its internal heat.

Stages of the solar system's formation are shown in the artist's impression below. The Sun formed from a gas cloud that shrank until it got so hot that nuclear reactions began in its core, making it glow. Debris around the Sun formed a disk of gas, dust, and ice, which gravity contracted to form planets.

Weather and Climate

If you took a tour through Jupiter's cloud layer, you would see weather as complex and spectacular as the weather on Earth. Jupiter has torrential rain, blizzards of snow, screaming winds, towering thunderstorms, and lightning bolts hundreds of times more powerful than any on Earth.

Clouds on Jupiter form similarly to Earth's but are made of different chemicals. High up in the **atmosphere,** the **hydrogen** air gets very cold. When the temperature gets low enough, gases condense into liquid droplets or freeze into ice crystals, which float in the air to form clouds. By studying the way the clouds reflect sunlight and the temperatures at which they form, three main cloud layers have been identified, from top to bottom: **ammonia** ice, ammonium hydrosulfide ice, and water ice.

As well as stormy weather, Jupiter has hot spots. These are high-pressure areas where creamy clouds disappear and reveal blue clouds below. Flying through a hot spot would be like emerging from a storm cloud into a sunny, tranquil area, with warmth rising from deep within the planet.

Cloud colors
*The chemicals in Jupiter's clouds are white, so where does all the color come from? Scientists think the answer must lie in other chemicals mixed up in the atmosphere. As the weather changes, clouds with different chemicals react with each other. **Sulfur**—which can take on colors from yellow to brown—may be involved.*

Earth's lightning (below) is dwarfed by that on Jupiter, where lightning bolts can reach 12,500 miles (20,000 kilometers) long.

A Day on Jupiter

You can't experience a day on Jupiter's surface because it doesn't have one, so you steer your ship toward a cloud and climb onto the roof. The first thing you notice is how heavy you feel—2.36 times your Earth weight. With a spacesuit on it's very difficult to stand up!

Jupiter **rotates** once every 9 hours 55 minutes, so its days are shorter than Earth's. At dawn the Sun rises quickly above the horizon, but because it's so far away its rays are weak. The cloud tops are a freezing –166°F (–110°C).

ABOVE: A solar eclipse happens when the Sun is blocked by a moon. This photograph shows the "diamond ring" effect that occurs toward the end of an eclipse, seen from Earth.

Later in the day the Sun disappears completely as one of Jupiter's moons passes in front of it, causing a total solar **eclipse.** In the eerie twilight, you see a vast bow of light across the sky—sunlight reflected off Jupiter's thin **rings.**

BELOW: Earth's aurora is caused by charged particles from the Sun striking gas molecules in the atmosphere.

As night falls you see colors in the sky—the **aurora.** This is caused by charged **particles** thrown out of volcanoes on Io, one of Jupiter's moons. The particles get trapped by Jupiter's **magnetic field** and smash into the **atmosphere,** making air **molecules** glow. They also produce radio waves, making the radio in your headset hiss.

Jupiter's Rings

gossamer ring

main ring

halo ring

The rings of Jupiter are much thinner and fainter than the famous rings of Saturn. Jupiter's rings are made of dust so fine that it looks like smoke. Although the dust particles are microscopic, they are moving very fast, **orbiting** Jupiter once every few hours at the breakneck speed of 65,000 miles per hour (105,000 kilometers per hour).

Jupiter's ring system is also simpler than Saturn's, with only three main parts. The most obvious part is the main ring. It stretches thousands of miles into space but is only a few miles thick. Wrapped around this like a sandwich is the faint gossamer ring. Closest to Jupiter is the halo ring, which, at its widest point, is about 12,000 miles (20,000 kilometers) thick, making it fat enough to swallow Earth.

Because the dust particles are very small they are slowed down by Jupiter's magnetic field and fall into the halo ring. From here they are gradually sucked into Jupiter's atmosphere, where they burn up. The rings are replenished by large boulders and small moons inside the ring system. These keep getting hit by **meteorites,** which release clouds of dust with each collision.

ABOVE: *Jupiter's rings consist of three main parts. Several tiny moons orbit within the rings.*

BELOW: *Only the main ring is visible to the naked eye from nearby. This photograph was taken by the* Galileo *probe when the Sun was behind Jupiter.*

The Jupiter System

Jupiter is a giant planet and has a huge family of moons to match—it's almost like a solar system in miniature. Astronomers have named 16 **Jovian** moons, which divide neatly into four groups of four. Closest in are four small moons that **orbit** inside Jupiter's **rings**: Metis, Adrastea, Amalthea, and Thebe. Then come four much larger moons, each thousands of miles across. These are the Galilean moons: Io, Europa, Ganymede, and Callisto. Far beyond the Galilean moons, some 7 million miles (11 million kilometers) from Jupiter, is the third group: Leda, Himalia, Lysithea, and Elara. These small, rocky moons have tilted orbits around Jupiter. Leda is only 10 miles (16 kilometers) wide, making it the smallest Jovian moon. Finally, some 14 million miles (22 million kilometers) from Jupiter, is the last group of moons: Ananke, Carme, Pasiphae, and Sinope. These are also small and rocky, and their orbits are highly stretched and tilted. Unlike the rest of Jupiter's moons, they orbit the planet in a clockwise direction.

Astronomers think Jupiter's moons formed in different ways. The inner eight moons seem to be made of similar materials—the same mix of rock and ice that might form the inner **core** of Jupiter. These moons probably formed from material left over after Jupiter's formation, just as the planets formed from leftovers of the Sun's formation. The Galilean moons grew large because they formed where the dust and ice was thickest.

The moons
This diagram shows the locations of Jupiter's sixteen moons. All their names come from characters in Greek mythology.

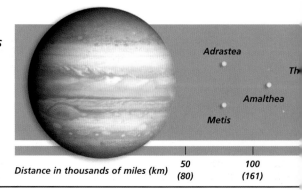

Adrastea

Th

Amalthea

Metis

Distance in thousands of miles (km)   50 (80)   100 (161)

The inner moons remained small because when they tried to combine, Jupiter's **gravity** pulled them apart again.

The eight outer moons are very different. Small and oddly shaped, their compositions and colors vary, and their orbits are peculiar. These factors suggest that they are **asteroids** caught in orbits around Jupiter. One theory is that the young Jupiter's powerful gravity disrupted the orbits of asteroids across a huge stretch of space between today's **asteroid belt** and Saturn's orbit, and captured a few of them. This explains the odd orbits of these outer moons and why they are so different from each other.

Jupiter's family of moons are trapped by the massive planet's gravity. This artist's impression shows four of the moons: Europa (left), Io (top), Ganymede (right), and Callisto (bottom).

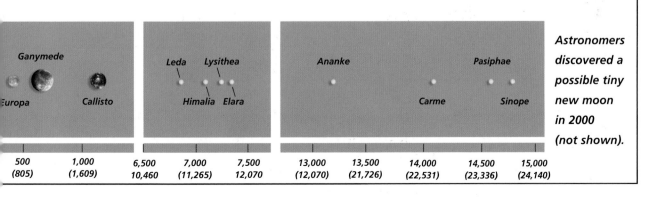

Astronomers discovered a possible tiny new moon in 2000 (not shown).

			Leda	Lysithea		Ananke			Pasiphae	
Ganymede										
Europa		Callisto		Himalia	Elara			Carme		Sinope
500 (805)	1,000 (1,609)		6,500 10,460	7,000 (11,265)	7,500 12,070	13,000 (12,070)	13,500 (21,726)	14,000 (22,531)	14,500 (23,336)	15,000 (24,140)

The Galilean Moons

The Galilean moons were created from fragments of rock and ice that were left over after Jupiter itself formed. These pieces of **debris** around Jupiter collided into each other, sticking together to make clumps that gradually grew into moons. The collisions caused the moons' interiors to heat up, and the inner three moons—Io, Europa, and Ganymede—got hot enough to melt on the inside. Heavier rock and metal sank toward the centers, while lighter materials rose to the surface, giving the moons **dense** metallic **cores** and lighter outer layers.

It is strange that Jupiter's moon Callisto never developed a metallic core, since it is Jupiter's second-largest moon and large worlds usually heat up the most during their formation. Likewise, small moons are usually cold worlds with little geological activity, yet the small moon Io is covered with active volcanoes.

The answer to these puzzles probably lies in the fact that the Galilean moons are close to Jupiter and close to each other. The inner moons are caught in a gravitational tug of war between Jupiter and the outer moons. As they **orbit** the planet they are pulled in different directions.

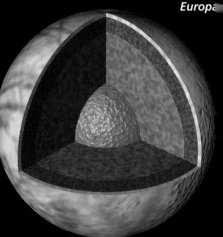

Europa

Europa's metallic core is covered by a layer of rock (brown). Surrounding this is a deep layer of water (blue), which may be either frozen or liquid. The crust is made of ice.

Size compared to Earth

Although smaller than Earth, all of the Galilean moons are bigger than the planet Pluto, and the largest of them—Ganymede—is bigger than Mercury. If these worlds were orbiting the Sun instead of Jupiter, we would call them planets instead of moons.

Earth

 Io

 Europa

 **Ganymede**

 **Callisto**

his process tugs them out of shape, which keeps
eir interiors hot and molten. The effect was
rong enough to melt the inner moons and
xplains why they have well-developed cores.
also explains why Ganymede has signs that it
nce had shifting **plates** in its **crust,** just like
arth. Only Callisto, the outermost moon, is a cold,
atered world, probably unchanged since it formed.

*Io's metallic core is surrounded by a
thick layer of molten rock that extends
nearly all the way to the surface.*

llisto

Ganymede

*llisto has no core. Most of the moon's
terior consists of rock and ice mixed
gether. The crust is made of ice.
tronomers think there might also be
 ocean (blue) below the crust.*

*Ganymede has four layers: an inner
core of iron, an outer core of rock
and iron, a deep layer of warm, soft
ice (blue), and a solid crust of ice.*

Io

The **Voyager 1** *space probe* *took this stunning picture of Io dwarfed by the Great Red Spot (left). The moon to the right is Europa.*

Firing up the rockets, you steer your ship toward Io, Jupiter's innermost moon. Approaching from the night side, you watch as the Sun's dazzling rays break over Io's horizon. Something is caught in the light—a faint, yellowish cloud of dust around Io. As the sunward side swings into view, the hazy dust vanishes and you see Io's amazing surface. Strange blotches of color all over Io make it look more like a pizza than a moon.

After landing and putting on your spacesuit, you climb down and stand on the surface. Io has almost no air, so the sky is always black and starry. The moon keeps the same face locked toward Jupiter all the time, so the giant planet hangs in the sky all day, looking truly spectacular—it is about 40 times the size of a full Moon from Earth.

Geysers

Unlike Earth's geysers (below), which shoot jets of scalding water into the air, Io's geysers eject jets of liquid sulfur. The sulfur freezes into "snow" as it escapes from the ground. Because Io has low gravity and little air, the geysers reach incredible heights, making them one of the most extraordinary sights in the solar system.

Now you can see where that dust came from. In front of you is a gigantic yellow fountain spurting hundreds of miles up and spreading at the top like an umbrella. It is a **geyser**—a jet of scalding liquid from underground. Earth has geysers too, but Io's are very different. They are far bigger, and the chemical they spurt out is **sulfur.**

You walk slowly toward the geyser, taking care not to take flying strides in Io's low **gravity.** Brown sulfur powder coats your boots as you crunch across the surface, and yellow sulfur snow starts falling as you get near the geyser. Before getting completely covered with sulfur you decide to return to the ship to take an aerial tour of Io.

As well as geysers, there are hundreds of active volcanoes on Io. Many have made made the ground collapse to form vast, sunken craters called **calderas,** and these have filled up with lava. In fact, Io is the most volcanically active world in the solar system. It has so many volcanoes and geysers that it is continually turning itself inside out and repainting its surface with sulfur. Sulfur ranges from yellow to brown and black when it cools, and this is how Io gets its color.

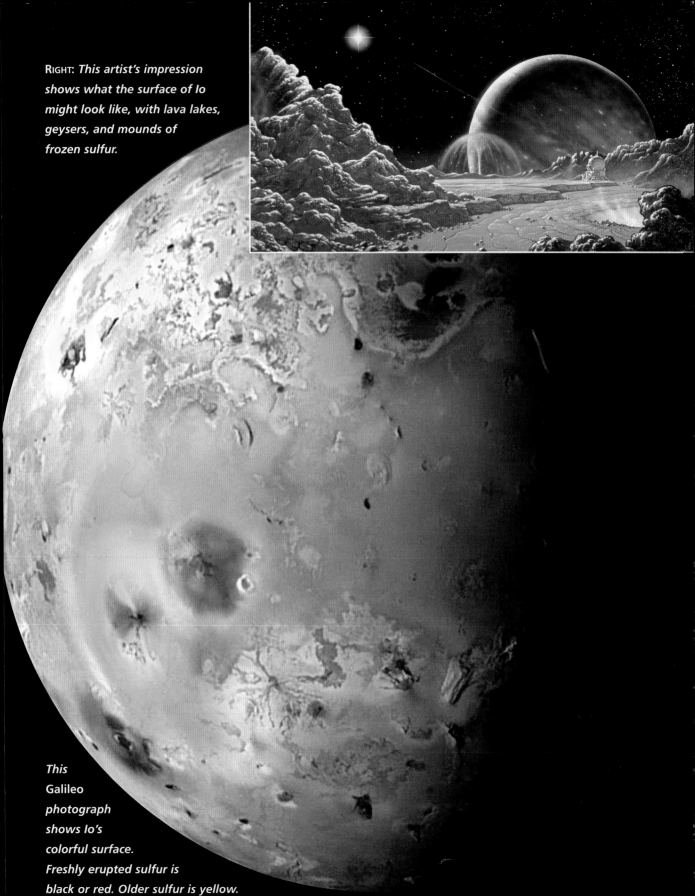

RIGHT: *This artist's impression shows what the surface of Io might look like, with lava lakes, geysers, and mounds of frozen sulfur.*

This Galileo photograph shows Io's colorful surface. Freshly erupted sulfur is black or red. Older sulfur is yellow.

Europa

Europa is the second Galilean moon, further from Jupiter and a little smaller than Io. From your spacecraft it looks bluish white, with hundreds of pink scratches. When it catches the light it dazzles you, and you find out why when you land—Europa is completely covered with ice.

The ice on Europa is so cold that it is rock solid and easy to walk on without slipping. You start to explore the landscape, again being careful to move slowly in the low **gravity.** Like Io, Europa is almost airless, and the only sounds you can hear are those coming from inside your spacesuit. You've landed in an area covered with icy ridges—just 30 or 40 feet (about 10 meters) high at most, but hundreds of miles long. You climb to the top of a ridge and look out over a much flatter icy plain beyond. Suddenly the ground shakes. A fountain of steam shoots up at the edge of the plain, before dying away in a shower of snowflakes.

As you've just experienced, Europa's ice keeps cracking, moving, and refreezing. This explains the long lines of ridges and cracks across the surface.

*The pink lines in this photo are fractures in Europa's **crust**. The white mark in the lower right is an enormous **impact crater**.*

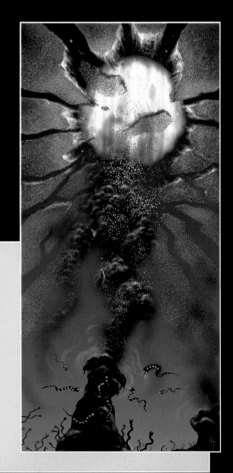

Life on Europa?

*In 1977 divers on Earth discovered warm undersea vents in the deepest and coldest oceans. These vents, called black smokers, are types of hot springs that release huge amounts of black, chemical-rich water into the sea. Many unusual forms of life have developed over time to live around them. Some scientists think that life on Earth may have begun around black smokers billions of years ago. If so, then could there also be life swimming around similar **sulfur**-belching vents in Europa's oceans (right)?*

It also explains why Europa has very few craters made by collisions with **comets** or **meteorites**. Like Io, it is constantly being resurfaced, and any craters get covered over. But why would the ice move like this, and where would the water come from? The most likely answer is that Europa's frozen surface must be hiding an ocean.

The idea that one of Jupiter's moons could have liquid water might seem ridiculous. But then Io should not logically have active volcanoes either. Astronomers think that the gravitational tug of war that keeps Io's interior molten also heats the inside of Europa. This means there could be volcanic activity under the surface, which would help keep the ocean warm. Perhaps Europa started out with a thick crust of ice and melted from the inside out, in which case its ocean might be as much as 100 miles (160 kilometers) deep. Where the moon's frozen surface cracks apart, water from the inside bubbles to the surface and freezes, resealing the crack and helping to protect the interior.

Finally, it's time to head back to the spacecraft. Before climbing aboard you take one last look at Jupiter, its magnificent disk hanging still over the horizon and casting a warm light across the endless ice.

ABOVE: *Seen from high above, Europa's icy surface is a maze of cracks and ridges.*

BELOW: *Jupiter looms on the horizon of Europa's ice-covered landscape in this artist's impression.*

Ganymede

Ganymede is the largest moon in the solar system and is bigger than the planets Pluto and Mercury. It is further from Jupiter than Io or Europa, but its surface still shows signs of an active history. As you fly past, you notice that there are two different types of surface on Ganymede: dark areas peppered with craters, and paler regions covered by ridges and valleys, but with fewer craters. The craters in the paler regions are a brilliant white—a clue that Ganymede has an icy interior.

Astronomers think the dark parts of Ganymede are rocky areas that have not changed for billions of years, which is why they have so many craters. In contrast, the pale regions are newer and seem to consist of ice that has welled up from deep inside the moon. Below Ganymede's surface is a shifting layer of ice warmed by heat from the **core**. As the ice circulates inside the moon, the surface of the paler regions stretches, forming ridges and valleys. Nobody knows whether this is still happening, or whether Ganymede has now frozen solid. The core is thought to be mostly iron and generates a weak **magnetic field** around Ganymede.

ABOVE: *The white marks on Ganymede are splashes of ice caused by violent collisions with **asteroids** and **comets**.*

BELOW: *Jupiter dominates the skyline over the moon Ganymede in this artist's impression.*

Callisto

The outermost Galilean moon is a dark world covered in brilliant white craters. Unlike the inner moons, Callisto never got hot enough to melt on the inside. But somehow it seems to have formed a hidden underground sea, like Europa.

The main clues about Callisto's interior come from its magnetic field. Unlike Ganymede, Callisto doesn't generate its own magnetic field, but it picks up magnetism from Jupiter (just as paperclips can pick up magnetism from a strong magnet). Scientists think this means that Callisto might have a hidden underground sea 6 to 60 miles (10 to 100 kilometers) deep, because a moon with a purely solid interior would not pick up any magnetism.

No one knows how such a sea could have formed, but it might explain the brilliance of Callisto's craters. If the impact of a **meteorite** is strong enough to gouge through Callisto's outer rocky layer, then water and ice from inside can well up to the surface and freeze over to heal the gap. The bright centers of large craters, formed in this way, are called **palimpsests.** The largest is at the center of Valhalla, an impact crater the size of Arizona. The collision that produced the Valhalla crater was so violent that it left ripples stretching halfway across Callisto's surface.

ABOVE: *The Valhalla crater, surrounded by vast, circular ripples, is at the bottom of this photograph of Callisto.*

BELOW: *Crater-covered Callisto was bombarded by comets, asteroids, and meteorites early in its history (artist's impression).*

Early Discoveries

The Romans named Jupiter after their king of the gods because they saw the planet as brilliant but slow-moving and stately. Jupiter was worshiped as the god of rain, thunder, and lightning, and the Romans built temples for him in places that were struck by lightning, such as the tops of hills. Astronomers from Roman to medieval times improved their understanding of Jupiter's movement in the skies, but they knew nothing about the planet itself.

ABOVE: *Galileo demonstrated his newly built telescope to the ruler of Venice in 1609. Galileo is shown in this engraving wearing a green coat.*

All this changed when Galileo discovered the four major moons of Jupiter in 1610. He was the first astronomer to look at Jupiter with a telescope, and his discoveries revolutionized astronomy.

At the time, most people believed that Earth was the center of the universe, and that everything else, including the Sun and the stars, **orbited** around it. In 1543 a Polish priest named Nicolaus Copernicus (1473–1543) had suggested that the Sun might be the center of the universe, but with nothing to back the theory up, his ideas were mostly ignored. Galileo's discovery of moons in orbit around an object other than Earth, and his other astronomical discoveries, provided the evidence to prove Copernicus was right.

The name Jupiter comes from a Roman god, shown here hurling a thunderbolt.

Galileo's discovery

Galileo published sketches of Jupiter's main moons in 1610 in a book called The Starry Messenger. *The sketches showed how the moons kept changing position. A German astronomer named Simon Marius claimed he had seen the moons first, but he was not taken seriously because he had a grudge against Galileo. However, we still call the moons by the names Marius gave them.*

ABOVE: *The Galilean moons are clearly visible from Earth with binoculars or a telescope.*

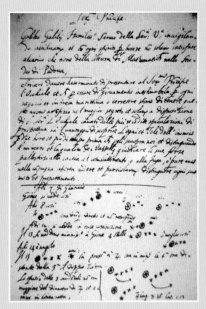

LEFT: *This page from* The Starry Messenger *shows the Galilean moons moving around Jupiter.*

The invention of the telescope turned the planets into worlds in their own right. Early telescopes could only magnify, but as they improved, astronomers started to see marks on the surface of Jupiter. At first they thought these might be islands, but gradually they realized that the changing patterns were most likely caused by clouds.

Astronomers were able to calculate Jupiter's distance from the Sun by measuring the length of its orbit, but discovering Jupiter's size took longer. They knew the planet had to be huge because it appeared so large in their telescopes, but it was not until 1750 that the English astronomer James Bradley (1693–1762) calculated Jupiter's **diameter** accurately. The planet's weight was not discovered until the 1920s.

The invention of photography in the 1800s had almost as much effect on astronomy as the invention of the telescope. Details could now be recorded over long periods of time without having to rely on the accuracy of a sketch. As a result, astronomers realized that the Great Red Spot was a permanent feature of the planet, and they devised a naming system for Jupiter's stripes. Photography also helped in the discovery of new moons.

Ole Romer
(1644–1710)

The Danish astronomer Ole Romer used Jupiter to calculate the speed of light. Romer noticed that **eclipses** *of Jupiter's moons occurred slightly later than predicted when Jupiter was furthest away from Earth in its orbit. He realized this was because light from the event was taking longer to reach us. He estimated the speed of light to be about 140,000 miles (225,000 kilometers) per second—a good guess, but slightly off. We now know the speed of light is 186,000 miles (300,000 kilometers) per second.*

Probes to Jupiter

Several **space probes** have visited Jupiter, and each has added to our knowledge about the planet and its moons. However, there are still mysteries to be solved, and more **missions** are planned.

The space shuttle Atlantis *launched* Galileo *on its six-year trip to Jupiter in October 1989.*

The first probes to visit Jupiter were *Pioneers 10* and *11* in 1973 and 1974. These high-speed probes, launched by NASA, reached Jupiter in less than two years and returned the first photos of the **Jovian** system as they flew past. They also measured Jupiter's enormous **magnetic field** and the **radiation belts** within the field.

The *Pioneers* were followed by *Voyagers 1* and *2* in 1979. These probes had improved cameras and sent back close-ups of the complex clouds on Jupiter and, for the first time, detailed pictures of the interesting moons. The probes discovered the smooth, icy surface of Europa, volcanoes on Io, and Jupiter's **ring** system, before flying on to the other outer planets.

But astronomers wanted a longer and more detailed look, particularly at Jupiter's moons. So, in 1989, the *Galileo* probe was launched on a slow journey that would not end with a flyby but would place the craft in **orbit** around Jupiter.

Galileo was an ambitious project and ran into trouble almost immediately, when the spacecraft's main radio dish failed to unfold properly.

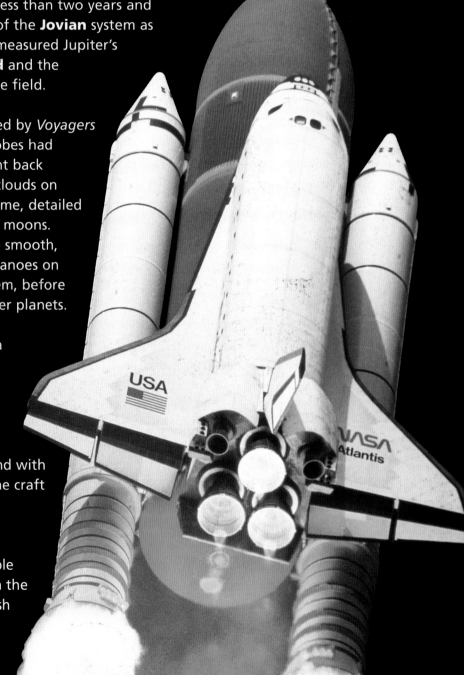

At first NASA engineers thought the mission was crippled. However, they found a way to send data back from the craft at a slower rate by using another dish, and the project was soon back on course.

The *Galileo* mission actually had two parts: an orbiting spacecraft, and an atmospheric probe designed to plunge into Jupiter's **atmosphere** to study conditions there. After the probe lost contact—crushed by Jupiter's atmosphere—the orbiter began its work.

The *Galileo* orbiter entered a complex orbit that took it over Jupiter's cloud tops and through a series of close encounters with the Galilean moons. The mission revolutionized some of our ideas about the Jupiter system—discovering a possible underground sea on Callisto and Europa, for example—and confirmed many theories. The orbiter is still working today, and scientists hope that it will continue to operate until 2003, when it will plunge into Jupiter's atmosphere and burn up. Its latest pictures can be seen on the Internet.

ABOVE: *The* Galileo *probe consisted of an atmospheric probe (above left) and an orbiter (above right).*

Future missions

The next probe to visit the Jupiter system will probably be NASA's Europa Orbiter, which will study the smallest of the Galilean moons. Astronomers are hoping to find signs that life could exist beneath the frozen surface. Perhaps later missions will send down landers to drill through the ice and explore the underground seas, as in this artist's impression (right).

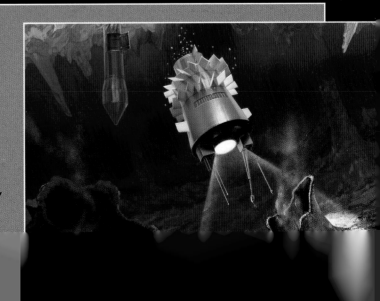

Comet Crash

In July 1994, while *Galileo* was still on its way to Jupiter, astronomers got the chance of a lifetime to look inside the planet when a **comet** crashed into it. Comets are vast lumps of ice that swoop around the solar system, sometimes ending up on a collision course with the Sun or the planets. They are famous for the spectacular white tails that they develop as they approach the Sun and their surface evaporates into space.

The comet that smashed into Jupiter was called Shoemaker-Levy 9 (SL9). Astronomers noticed something odd about SL9 soon after its discovery in 1993. It looked more like 21 separate comets strung out in a line than a single ball of ice, and it was racing headlong toward Jupiter. Once the comet's **orbit** had been determined it was obvious what had happened. SL9 had been captured by Jupiter's **gravity** during a close encounter with the planet in 1992. The force of Jupiter's attraction had torn the comet into a string of fragments and set it on its current path to destruction.

A comet crash is a rare event—something that happens once every few centuries at most.

Lᴇꜰᴛ: *The fragments of SL9 produced fireballs bigger than Earth as they struck Jupiter (artist's impression).*

For astronomers the Shoemaker-Levy crash was an amazing stroke of luck because it gave them a unique chance to study Jupiter's interior. As the fragments hit the planet, they would stir up Jupiter's **atmosphere** and bring materials from deep within the planet to the surface. Although the impacts would happen on the far side of Jupiter, the planet's **rotation** would quickly bring the impact sites into view.

For six days in July 1994, every available telescope was trained on Jupiter. The comet crash was the single most watched astronomical event ever, and the biggest explosion ever observed in the solar system. Some of the best pictures came from the Hubble Space Telescope, but the *Galileo* probe got the only direct view of the impact.

Huge plumes of gas rose thousands of miles above the explosion sites on the edge of Jupiter. By the time the sites came into view they were visible as dark bruises, but these were soon swallowed up by Jupiter's constantly swirling clouds. Astronomers had expected to find bright water clouds dredged up from the depths, but instead they detected the chemicals **sulfur** and hydrogen sulfide. It seems that the comet did not penetrate as far into Jupiter as was expected, but it was still a spectacular event.

Comet Hyakutake (above) is one of many comets that occasionally pass within sight of Earth. Scientists think Jupiter's gravity has a strong influence on the solar system's comets. It swallows some but flings others out into deep space, protecting Earth from the danger of impacts.

Eugene Shoemaker
(1928–1997)

Comet Shoemaker-Levy 9 was named after its discoverers, David Levy and Eugene and Carolyn Shoemaker. Eugene Shoemaker was a geologist who pioneered the study of the planets using geological techniques. The danger posed to Earth by comets was one of his major concerns, and Shoemaker-Levy 9 was just one of many comets he and his wife discovered.

Could Humans Live There?

One day the Jupiter system might be home to an outpost of humans, but this is a very distant prospect. Any **mission** to Jupiter would be a very long one, taking at least ten years. Jupiter itself is uninhabitable, but humans could live on a space station nearby. Or perhaps a permanent base could be built on one of the Galilean moons—but they are all forbidding environments, with no air, freezing surfaces, and deadly **radiation** levels. At least ice is plentiful and could be used for making water, oxygen, and fuel. But astronauts living in the Jupiter system would have to spend all their time in airtight, artificial surroundings.

If **space probes** ever find traces of life in the Jupiter system, then a mission to collect samples would have to be very carefully planned. Contamination with alien germs, which evolved in a very different environment to Earth, could prove fatal. It would be safest for humans to keep their distance completely and send only robots to investigate on our behalf.

Setting up a space station in the Jupiter system might be the first step in building a human base (artist's impression).

Glossary

ammonia chemical with the formula NH_3. It is found as ice in Jupiter's atmosphere

artificial gravity force generated by a spaceship that enables astronauts to stand on the floor instead of floating in midair. One way a spacecraft is able to create artificial gravity is to spin around.

asteroid large chunk of rock left over from when the planets formed

asteroid belt ring of asteroids that orbit the Sun between the orbits of Mars and Jupiter

astronaut person trained to go into space

atmosphere layer of gas trapped by gravity around the surface of a planet

atom minute particle of matter

aurora colorful glow in the sky caused by charged particles hitting the atmosphere

axis imaginary line through the middle of a planet that the planet spins around

brown dwarf object smaller than a star yet larger than a planet that produces light but not heat

caldera large crater formed by the collapse of a volcano

comet large chunk of ice left over from when the planets formed. It develops a long, glowing tail of gas and dust as it nears the Sun.

core center of a planet or moon where the heaviest elements have collected

crescent curved shape like one segment of an orange

crust solid outer surface of a planet or moon, where the lighter elements have collected

debris fragments of rock, dust, ice, or other materials floating in space

dense having a lot of weight squeezed into a small space

diameter length of an object measured by drawing a straight line through its center

eclipse effect caused by a planet or moon moving in front of the Sun and casting a shadow on another object

element chemical that cannot be split into other chemicals

geyser eruption of scalding liquid and steam from underground

gravity force that pulls objects together. The heavier or closer an object is, the stronger is its pull, or gravity.

helium second most common element in the universe. Helium is one of the gases in Jupiter's atmosphere.

hemisphere top or bottom half of a planet, moon, or star

hydrogen simplest, lightest, and most common element in the universe. Hydrogen is the fuel that makes stars shine. It makes up most of the gas in the Sun and in the planets Jupiter and Saturn.

impact crater circular crater made when an asteroid, comet, or meteorite smashes into a planet or moon

Jovian relating to the planet Jupiter

lander spacecraft that lands on a moon or planet

magnetic field region around a planet where a compass can detect the north pole

mantle part of a planet or moon located between the core and the crust

meteorite rock from space that falls onto the surface of a planet or moon

mission expedition to visit a specific target in space, such as a planet or moon

molecule tiny unit of matter consisting of two or more atoms joined together

north pole point on the surface of a planet moon, or star that coincides with the top end of its axis

orbit path an object takes around another when it is trapped by the larger object's gravity; or, to take such a path

palimpsest bright, frozen center of a large impact crater, made up of water and ice that welled up from inside the planet or moon.

particle tiny fragment of an atom. Particle can also mean a speck of dust or dirt.

plate part of the crust of planet or moon that moves about and collides with other plates

plume volcanic geyser of sulfur erupting on Jupiter's moon Io

radiation energy released in rays from a source. Heat and light are types of radiation.

radiation belt region around a planet where the magnetic field traps radiation from the Sun

ring circle made up of millions of ice or rock particles orbiting together around a planet

rotate to turn about an object's center, or axis

satellite an object that orbits a planet

space probe robotic vehicle sent from Earth to study the solar system

sulfur element that has several different forms and colors

More Books to Read

Berger, Melvin. *Discovering Jupiter: The Amazing Collision in Space.* New York: Scholastic, 1995.

Bond, Peter. *DK Guide to Space.* New York: Dorling Kindersley, 1999.

Couper, Heather, and Henbest, Nigel. *The DK Space Encyclopedia.* New York: Dorling Kindersley, 1999.

McDonald, Mary Ann. *Jupiter: Our Universe Series.* Chanhassen, Minn.: Child's World, 1997.

Simon, Seymour. *The Solar System.* New York: William Morrow, 1992.

Index

Picture Credits
Key: t – top, b – below, c – center, l – left, r – right. **NASA**: 2t, 2b, 3, 4–5b, 7, 7b, 9l, 9r, 10, 11b, 12t, 12b, 13t, 13b, 19t, 19b, 20–21, 22t, 22bl, 22br, 23t, 23c, 23b, 24t, 25b, 26t, 27t, 28t, 29t, 31tc, Don Davis 33t, R. Evans/J. Trauger/H. Hammel/HST Comet Science Team 34t, JPL/California Institute of Technology 1, 27b, 33b; **SOHO***: 4l; **Corbis**: Araldo de Luca 30b; **Science Photo Library**: 21t, 30t, Julian Baum 34b, Dr Jeremy Burgess, Chris Butler 28b, Mark Garlick 16, 29b, David Hardy 11t, 15t, 25t, 26b, Roger Harris 36, Adam Hart-Davis 15b, Keith Kent 24b, NASA 8b, 32, David Parker 35b, Pekka Parviainen 18b, Rev. Ronal Royer 18t, 31tr, John Sanford 8t, John Thomas 35t, Kent Wood 17. Front Cover: NASA. Back Cover: NASA, JPL/California Institute of Technology.
*SOHO is a project of international cooperation between ESA & NASA.